# Brigadier John Tiltman: A Giant Among Cryptanalysts

Center for Cryptologic History

National Security Agency

2007

*This publication is a product of the National Security Agency history program. It presents a historical perspective for informational and educational purposes, is the result of independent research, and does not necessarily reflect a position of NSA/CSS or any other U.S. government entity*

Brigadier John Tiltman has been variously described as the greatest cryptanalyst of his time, the best cryptanalyst ever to work for Government Communications Headquarters (GCHQ, Great Britain's counterpart to NSA), and a "legend in his own time." He led the attack on numerous code and cipher systems of over a dozen countries. At the same time, he developed cipher systems for his own country that were unbreakable during the time they were used. He held the title of Chief Cryptographer for the Government Code and Cypher School (GC&CS, which became GCHQ in 1946) from 1942 on. He humbly described this position as "honorary," but it carried the dual responsibility of being tasked with the initial diagnosis of and attack on all unbroken foreign cipher systems, and the development of secure ciphers for British forces.

His career spanned two world wars, conflicts in Korea and Vietnam, and most of the Cold War. Retiring from GCHQ in 1964, he capitalized on relations he had built up over the previous two decades and served as a consultant to NSA until 1980. At the age of eighty-five, he finally stepped away from sixty-six years of public service to two countries. Sixty of those years were devoted to signals intelligence (SIGINT) and communications security (COMSEC). To those who worked with him, he was known simply as "The Brig."

## Early Years

John Hessell Tiltman was born in London on 25 March 1894. He attended Charterhouse School and early on showed the intellectual prowess that would mark his career. At age thirteen, he was offered a place at Oxford. He was unable to accept the position because the recent death of his father had changed the family's circumstances to a degree that made attendance at university a luxury they could not afford. Upon leaving school in 1911, he became a teacher, another early indication of a lifelong tendency, this one to educate those around him.

Whatever aspirations Tiltman had towards a "normal" life of teaching and continued learning were interrupted abruptly, as were the varied ambitions of his generation, by the outbreak of World War I in 1914. Heeding the call of patriotism that moved millions across the European continent, he enlisted in September 1914. He received a temporary commission (which became permanent in 1916) in the King's Own Scottish Borderers. He served with distinction, being wounded in 1917 and receiving the Military Cross for valor.

In 1919, while still recovering from his wounds, he was attached to the British Military Mission that was sent to Irkutsk in Siberia. At that time Britain, along with several other of the recently victorious allies (including France, the U.S., and Japan) sent contingents of troops to parts of Russia following the Bolshevik Revolution in October/November 1917. Their purpose was twofold: to keep supplies the allies had sent to the tsarist government for the common fight against Germany from falling into Bolshevik hands, and to support the counterrevolutionary forces (White Russians) formed to overthrow the newly established Communist (Red) regime. Tiltman believed that he was selected because he had picked up a smattering of Russian during his teaching days.

His Siberian tour was cut short because he had not yet fully recovered from his war wounds. He estimated that he was able to spend only about six weeks actually working out of the two and a half months he spent in Russia. The fact that he undertook to inspect a course set up to train officers for the White armies, a task that involved an eight-mile roundtrip walk in the dead of Siberian winter (with temperatures around sixty-one degrees below zero Fahrenheit, and a stiff wind to boot) did nothing to improve his health. In fact, it led to his being hospitalized in Vladivostok. From there he was evacuated back to Britain.

Nonetheless, this brief tour allowed him to reinforce his language skills sufficiently to be selected to attend a Russian course for Army officers at King's College in London starting in March 1920. Tiltman never considered himself to be a linguist, as he found languages hard to acquire, but he was far enough ahead of his fellow students that he spent most of the course teaching himself and not actually attending class. At the conclusion of the course, he tested successfully as a second-class interpreter. This success would, under normal circumstances, have entitled him to a three-year tour in Russia to hone his newly acquired skills. Great Britain and the nascent Soviet Union did not, however, have diplomatic relations, so such a tour was out of the question.

Instead, he was seconded to the War Office and sent to work at GC&CS to help deal with a backlog of Russian diplomatic decrypts. GC&CS had been formed after World War I from the naval effort in the Admiralty and the military one at the War Office. When Tiltman joined, it was located in Watergate House on the Thames Embankment near Charing Cross. Its head, who would serve until 1945, was A. G. Denniston. His deputy was E. W. Travis, who would replace Denniston as head of the Bletchley Park effort in 1942 and continue until 1952. Tiltman's secondment was to have lasted for two weeks. It resulted in a career change that lasted for sixty years.

Tiltman quickly demonstrated a proficiency in dealing with Russian ciphers, so the two-week assignment was extended at first to a year during which time he slowly evolved from an interpreter into a cryptanalyst. He worked under the direction and tutelage of Ernst Fetterlein, an amazing story in his own right. Fetterlein had been the chief cryptanalyst for the Russian tsarist government, holding the ranks of both admiral and general. Following the Bolshevik Revolution, he walked across the Finnish border and made his way to Great Britain where he became a naturalized British citizen and went to work for GC&CS.

In Tiltman, Fetterlein must have recognized a kindred spirit. Tiltman later recalled that Fetterlein took him under his wing. He became the only person (in an office of six or seven) the Russian would actually take the time to train in cryptanalysis. Even then, there was no formal training involved, just useful hints on how to identify types of ciphers and attacks that would prove useful against them. It was all very much in the nature of on-the-job training. In later years, Tiltman in a way repaid the debt he owed his early mentor. In 1935 he recruited Ernst's brother to work for GC&CS, and also brought the brother's son into the business.

Tiltman later described the Russian ciphers he dealt with as low-grade simple columnar transposition systems with key that changed with each message. In 1921 the Russians changed the system and began using dinome substitution underneath the transposition. Since they continued using the old keys, the system broke fairly easily.

Then in March they introduced an entirely new system with new keys, and some effort was required to break in. The British were assisted by a lazy code clerk (not the last time Tiltman would be able to use this advantage), who, in effect, defeated the system by not using all the possible variants available to him. The system was built so that each vowel could be substituted for by seven different dinomes that would reduce the chance that repetitions would reveal the frequency count cryptanalysts use to wedge their way into a cipher. In one particular message, however, a single word (the Russian *dogovor*, "treaty") appeared multiple times. Each time, the less-than-diligent clerk used the same vowel dinomes rather than the variants. With that edge, Tiltman worked out the cipher system.

His next lesson in the world of ciphers involved finding the method used to determine the transposition keys so that exploitation could become essentially routine. It soon became clear that the keys were derived from lines of poetry, but it took some time to uncover that the author was an obscure mid-seventeenth century English poet. Tiltman then had to find the book or anthology that was being used. Through resourceful digging he found the book, an out-of-print edition of the poet's works held by the British Museum. That venerable institution then invoked a strict interpretation of the law which forbade removal of works it held to block the request of GC&CS to borrow the book and copy it, questions of national security notwithstanding. It took the personal intervention of the director of GC&CS to convince the British Museum to allow a one-shilling book (a shilling being $1/20^{th}$ of a British pound and worth at that time about 50 cents in U.S. currency) to be borrowed, even though this was "breaking the law of the land."

## Tour in India

Then, in September 1921, Tiltman was assigned to the General Staff of British Indian Army Headquarters in Simla, India, to replace the officer in charge, one Colonel Jeffery. The original intent had been to post Tiltman as the assistant military attaché in Meshed, Iran, where an effort was already under way to exploit Russian ciphers. This posting would have involved mostly translation work. The British powers-that-be realized that this would be a waste of the cryptanalytic talents Tiltman was already demonstrating. So plans were altered, he went to Simla, and the Meshed project was dropped. He was to remain in this position as an army captain until 1925. Following the first of what would prove to be numerous retirements, he continued doing the same job as a War Office civil servant (with the title "Signal Computor") until 1929.

In his new posting, Tiltman had to overcome unexpected opposition. The original intent had been that he would replace Colonel Jeffery since that officer had opted to retire rather than face a mandatory posting to the regiment he nominally belonged to, but in which he had never actually served. While Tiltman was en route to Simla, Jeffery changed his mind and opted to remain in the service. His decision was made easy since the British Army elected to allow him to remain in his job at Simla and not force a return to his regiment (one can imagine that the regiment itself felt some relief with this change of heart since it would have been put in the position of receiving a senior officer who knew nothing of its traditions and practices). When Tiltman arrived, tension between the two was almost instinctive.

Jeffery had begun his career by spending three years in China, "gone native" as the British used to put it. He traveled extensively throughout the country becoming, in the process, a first-rate Chinese linguist and scholar. He was then posted to South Africa and placed in charge of Chinese coolies working in the mines there. In 1912 he landed in India on the intelligence staff. There, without any formal training, he built up a library on Chinese codes. Having worked for years in isolation on the Chinese problem, he believed he had essentially invented the process of breaking into Chinese systems on his own. Into his world now stepped Tiltman, who later admitted that his own brashness and conceit did nothing to smooth the transition. Jeffery left for a year's leave with the two barely on speaking terms. The situation did not improve upon his return in 1922, and friction between the old hand and the new "upstart" threatened to disrupt the entire mission. Tiltman learned to keep his distance, a task made easier since his work involved Russian intercept. Jeffery preferred to continue working Chinese systems, and adamantly refused to learn Russian.

Over the next several years, the two learned to overcome their initial differences and developed a respect for each other's professional skills. Jeffery would eventually be forced into retirement in 1935, suffering from double cataracts. With tensions mounting in Europe in 1938, his skills were needed, and it was Tiltman who persuaded him to return to service, this time with Tiltman as senior, in spite of misgivings on Jeffery's part that his recently repaired eyesight (he had had the cataracts surgically removed by 1938) might suffer from the strain of cryptologic work. It is a tribute to both men that they had overcome whatever differences plagued their initial relationship to the point where they liked and respected each other enough to put their skills to work for the greater good.

During the assignment in Simla, Tiltman sharpened the skills that would make him one of Britain's premier cryptanalysts. The job was to gather and analyze Russian diplomatic messages being sent between Moscow, Tashkent, and Kabul. Given the small size of the British effort (never more than five individuals in the 1920s), Tiltman became involved in all aspects of the problem. This included directing the intercept, encouraging the intercept operators at various collection sites on the Northwest Frontier, performing rudimentary traffic analysis, diagnosing the cipher systems (which frequently changed), stripping the long additive keys, recovering the underlying code books, translating the messages, and then arguing the significance of the messages with the Intelligence Branch. In addition, he wrote not only reports on individual events, but also summary reports. In short, circumstances led him to become proficient in virtually every aspect of the SIGINT business.

In later life, he insisted that this broad-based background was key to his further development, and gave him a deep appreciation for all aspects of the cryptologic problem. Though he came to recognize that modern specialization had its place, and made experiences such as his virtually impossible to replicate, he felt that younger generations of cryptanalysts could only suffer a loss of proficiency as a result.

Throughout this period, the Russians continually upgraded the cipher systems they were using, becoming increasingly sophisticated in their use of additives. The British, led by Tiltman, were able to keep up with the changes until 1928 when the Soviets introduced one-time pads, and their systems became essentially unreadable. He later recalled a couple of memorable incidents stemming from his successful efforts. In 1925 the British were facing another in a never-ending series of incidents along the Northwest Frontier, this time in Waziristan (located on the present-day border between Pakistan and Afghanistan), and mounted an expedition to deal with the problem. This prompted a message from the Soviet ambassador in Afghanistan to Moscow asking for instructions. The message was translated (and forwarded to British authorities in India) as asking what the Soviets contemplated doing "with a view to the occupation of Waziristan."

The implication that the Soviets might intend to send troops into an area the British considered their own raised the collective blood pressure in New Delhi and Simla. Fortunately those in charge realized the logistical impossibilities involved in moving forces rapidly over the Hindu Kush (the mountain range that effectively separates Afghanistan from Pakistan), and asked that the message be rechecked. That task fell to Tiltman, whose language skills were admittedly inferior to those of the original translator, but whose attention to detail and standards of accuracy were infinitely greater. He quickly recognized that the proper translation was "in view of the occupation of Waziristan." In other words, the ambassador wanted to know how Moscow wished him to react to the British occupation. Blood pressures returned to normal, and Tiltman now had an extra job, that of checking and correcting all Russian translations coming out of the effort in Simla.

The second incident involved a lost opportunity. The British learned that the Soviets had two cipher clerks in Kabul, Kotlov and Serafimovich. Because of recurring accuracy problems the Soviets experienced with the two, an order came down from Moscow insisting that all messages be signed in cipher by the clerk responsible for enciphering and sending the message. This provided Tiltman with a very useful crib for breaking into the ciphers used. Eventually, however, a message was intercepted instructing Serafimovich to return to Moscow since his papers were not in order. In the Soviet Union of 1926, there could be only one outcome of such a summons, and Serafimovich was well aware of what it would be. He fled at once to the British embassy, but was promptly ejected. Tiltman notes that he was never heard from again. Tiltman lost a useful message string that he had been using to break into Russian messages. The British lost the opportunity of debriefing an individual who had intimate knowledge of the various ciphers in use by the Soviets.

As if his various responsibilities on the SIGINT side of the business were not enough, Tiltman was also charged with creating practical ciphers for British use. He created a system that he believed was secure, improving on systems already in use. Typical of the man, however, was his continued study of the problem and eventual recognition that he had built flaws into his system which could be exploited. He used this lesson for two purposes. First, it allowed him to strengthen future systems he would be called on to create. He often pointed out that during the years when he was asked to create ciphers, no organized process existed to test the strength of any system before it was put into use. Only the diligence of the maker and his determination to follow up on his creation made the difference between a cipher that was vulnerable to exploitation and one whose weaknesses could be recognized and fixed.

The second advantage he gained was that he was able to use the knowledge he acquired to attack similar systems built by adversaries. He maintained that sloppy thinking would reveal itself faster in the development of ciphers than in just about any other field. Because of that, he found the practice of building ciphers to be useful in training the imagination for the diagnosis of complicated problems. One of his fundamental beliefs was that the livelihood of a cryptanalyst depends almost entirely on the overingenuity of the designers of foreign ciphers.

## Creation of the Military Section, GC&CS

In 1930 Tiltman was called back to Britain to set up the Military Section of GC&CS. The effort started with two permanent staff including Tiltman, and three trainee regular officers who were seconded to GC&CS for tours ranging from three to four years generally before deployment to the main Army Middle East station, at Sarafand in Palestine. Eventually, clerical support came in the form of the wives of the officers assigned to the section. While it was hoped that this would be a temporary solution, the help turned out to be more transitory than expected. The assistance of most of the wives lasted only a few months. A notable exception was Tiltman's own wife, Tempe, who stayed on until 1939.

The War Office had pushed to have this section created with the intent that it would concentrate its efforts on working against military ciphers. Due to limited collection resources, and the state of European relationships in the early 1930s, there was an extremely limited amount of military-related intercept available for use (to include training), so Tiltman resorted to gathering traffic that the other sections in GC&CS had either no time for or no interest in. This insistence on working whatever material was available, even if it had nothing to do with the military, led to some difficulties with the War Office. He pushed ahead, able to see that having cryptanalysts experienced at working with high-grade cipher systems would prove beneficial in the future. He would just have to allow the passage of time to convince those in the War Office who disagreed with the logic of his arguments.

As a result, he spent a good deal of time from 1931 to 1935 working Comintern (the Communist International, an organization established by Moscow to control worldwide communist parties) traffic. The network his section was interested in was centered in Berlin, with links to London, Paris, Amsterdam, Vienna, Rome, and some locations in the Far East. They also exploited a related Moscow-to-Berlin link. The network used a codebook plus novels to generate running key for encipherment purposes. So once again, as at the beginning of his cryptologic career, Tiltman found himself in the hunt for obscure literary works. His group found that the books used were primarily in German, though the London link used English language novels and collections of poetry.

Eventually, through many trips to book dealers and libraries in London, Berlin, Amsterdam, and other European cities, Tiltman tracked down the various books used by the London link and several used by the others in the network as well. He noted that one particular problem he encountered on more than one occasion involved a difference in editions. He and his group kept assuming that the books used in London would be British editions. It turned out that in some instances the Comintern agents opted to use American editions. These generally had different pagination and even, in the case of poetry collections, contained different poems.

His work paid off, however, as it provided insight into Comintern efforts (or at least wishful thoughts, as very little subversion was ever actually proven) aimed at subverting members of the British armed forces. Efforts were made, successfully in the final analysis, to locate the British end of these transmissions. The effort was hindered by the fairly primitive direction finding equipment available at the time. Nonetheless, A.G. Denniston, head of GC&CS, considered this effort to be his organization's most successful operation of the 1930s.

His work on this problem led to his initial contacts with the French, and here he gave a preview of the skills that would later serve him so well in establishing a close working relationship with the Americans. He was sent to Paris to discuss mutual exploitation of Russian ciphers, but was instructed to avoid giving away anything the British had learned about Russian use of long additive streams or one-time pads. As he and the leader of the French contingent, Gustave Bertrand, were about to begin the ritual dance to determine who knew what, Bertrand immediately indicated that he knew where British sensitivities lay. He handed Tiltman a paper that contained exactly what the French knew, setting aside any qualms Tiltman's instructions may have caused. Tiltman responded to this openness in kind, and a relationship was established that served the British well throughout the decade as both countries grappled with matters of more immediate concern than Russian Comintern intrigues. The cooperation established in this exchange led to frank exchanges in dealing with the German Enigma machine.

The work done against the Comintern network, as indeed all of the cryptologic work done through the 1930s and in later years by Tiltman, was done by hand, with virtually no machine assistance. Tiltman remembered that in 1931-32 he had been asked by Denniston to visit the British Tabulating Machinery Company (BTM, the British licensee for IBM) to investigate the work they were doing on machines that might have a cryptologic application, especially in the field of sorting large volumes of data. He was singularly unimpressed, largely because the machines were so primitive that he could outperform them. He later admitted that this caused him to fail to recognize their potential, and to dismiss them. In his view, GC&CS delayed beginning to work with and influence the development of machines that would eventually lead to the computer age until the issue was forced on it at the beginning of World War II. This probably represents an oversimplification on his part, as other sections of GC&CS, and Tiltman himself, worked closely with BTM and others, setting the stage for its great successes against German machine systems during the war.

As the 1930s progressed, the international scene shifted to one that was more threatening. The decade began with Britain facing an impoverished and disarmed Germany while being allied with the continent's dominant military force, France, as well as with Italy, at least nominally. The Soviet Union, while posing a rhetorical threat, was in the throes of a series of domestic turmoils that included collectivization, rapid industrialization, and seemingly endless internecine purges. These effectively rendered her, temporarily at least, a nonfactor in European power politics. In the Far East, Japan's expansionistic tendencies had not yet taken on an overt aggressiveness outside of Manchuria. The presence of elements of the British fleet in the region appeared to have that situation well under control.

By mid-decade, however, the situation had changed dramatically. Germany was in the control of the rabidly nationalistic National Socialist (Nazi) party, and had embarked on aggressive rearmament, denouncing the treaty system that had ended World War I. Italy had begun a policy of expansion into areas that threatened British communication with essential parts of her empire. Japanese expansive ambitions in the Pacific could no longer be disguised or complacently ignored. France still appeared to be the dominant military force in Europe, but her position was being increasing undermined by economic depression and internal political turmoil.

What this meant for Tiltman and his Military Section at GC&CS was that there was no longer a dearth of material with which to work, although the communications practices of the German forces meant that British interception of messages enciphered using the version of the Enigma machine adopted by the German

General Staff was limited. Tiltman conducted some investigations, solving the indicator system used by the Germans, but (unlike the Polish cryptanalysts led by Marian Rejewski) neither he nor his colleagues successfully attacked the machine itself. The British enjoyed some success against a less complicated variant of the Enigma used by Italian and Fascist forces during the Spanish Civil War. The major player in this effort was Alfred Dillwyn ("Dilly") Knox. Tiltman himself meanwhile began to concentrate on Japanese systems. There was still a general lack of German traffic, and Italian systems were handled by others in his section. It was, in fact, Italian military action, in Ethiopia (Abyssinia) in 1935, that led to the first expansion of the section with the addition of three officers, one an Italian linguist.

With others in his section dealing with the Italian problem, Tiltman was left free to concentrate on Japanese systems, particularly those used by Japanese military attachés. In 1933 he solved a system the attachés had been using since 1927. To do this, he had to teach himself the rudiments of Japanese on the fly, as it were. His success ran him head on into a prejudice he would reencounter during World War II. Prior to his breakthrough, the problem had been in the hands of two classically educated retired career diplomats who had served in Japan as consuls general and who knew the language. They had some degree of difficulty accepting that Tiltman, a self-taught linguistic amateur who had never set foot in Japan, could succeed where they had failed.

Tiltman moved on to work other Japanese military systems, concentrating on army traffic which was being provided by British sites in Hong Kong. His innate skills were complemented by Japanese misuse of their systems, and this enabled him to break first the indicating system in use and then the additive systems used to encipher the underlying code. By 1937 he believed that he had made enough progress in the system that it could be handed over to others to work. Particularly, he wanted the Far East Combined Bureau (the British joint service codebreaking and intelligence center, then in Hong Kong) to take up the work since they were closer to the immediate customer of the resulting product. The

Japanese practice of changing the substitution tables that were the heart of their system every six to nine months coupled with the inexperience and lack of confidence of the individuals in Hong Kong frustrated his plans for the moment.

Not every venture of his at this time was an unqualified success. Years later he enjoyed telling the story of how in 1935 he spent weeks working on what he thought was a batch of Japanese military intercepts forwarded by Hong Kong. He quickly established that he was working on unenciphered code, and began to break out the groups that stood for numbers. He found it curious that the numerical order of the code groups followed the stroke order in which the corresponding Chinese characters were written. He was hard at work, and quite a ways along, feeling good about his progress, when a friend who was a Chinese interpreter at the War Office looked at what he had and told him that he had just "broken" the publicly available Chinese Standard Telegraph Code (the telegraphic code used to render Chinese ideograms into text that could be sent over the "wires"). The experience was not lost on him, as we shall see.

On a more serious note, Tiltman continued his work against Japanese systems, moving to naval cipher systems in 1939. In that year he broke the additive system used by the latest Japanese Navy system, which would come to be designated JN-25 by the Western allies. This enabled him to begin stripping the cipher from the underlying code groups. Recovery of those code groups was then necessary before the actual messages could be read, and that process, as we shall see, was equally daunting. He credited his success to similarities between the naval additive system and the military ones which he had been successfully exploiting for several years.

A historical aside is called for at this point. Students of American cryptology are well aware that U.S. Navy cryptologists of OP-20-G were also independently working on Japanese naval codes and ciphers. Their effort suffered from extremely limited resources and was marked by hesitant success up to and through the Japanese attack on Pearl Harbor. Reading the JN-25 code would have provided invaluable insight into Japanese naval plans for that attack, just as it provided the key intelligence that enabled the U.S. Navy to plan its successful ambush of the Japanese Imperial Fleet at Midway in 1942.

Tiltman's breakthrough against JN-25 in 1939 should not be seen as food for the conspiracy theorists, who believe, among other things, that Britain had foreknowledge of the Pearl Harbor attack which was withheld so as to draw the U.S. into the fight. Breaking through the additive system used for encipherment (Tiltman's accomplishment, achieved independently by U.S. cryptanalysts as well) was just the first step needed for full exploitation of the information contained in Japanese naval messages. The underlying codebook then had to be recovered, a tedious and painstaking process where the progress of months of work could be and was undone in an instant by changing the book. Work could also be set back by changing the additive keybook used to encipher the code. The Japanese Navy was appropriately security conscious and changed its codebooks and its additive keys periodically (the actual codebook was revised once, the additive book six times between the time JN-25 was introduced and Pearl Harbor). This forced U.S. and British analysts to start from zero when the codebook was changed and set them back, though not as severely, each time the additive book was changed. Neither of the soon-to-be Anglo-Saxon allies had made sufficient progress into the codebook in use in late 1941 to predict the attack on Pearl Harbor (less than ten percent of the 50,000 entries in the codebook then in use had been recovered).

The year 1939 also marked Tiltman's success in an endeavor he had been working at since 1937. In that year he was finally able to shift responsibility for day-to-day work on the Japanese military systems to Hong Kong. He had come to find that keeping up with the changes the Japanese made every few months was consuming too much time, and his efforts were hampered by the lack of Japanese linguists assigned to the problem. He had solved the underlying technique. The everyday exploitation could now be handed over to individuals who were both closer to those who needed the intelligence and more adept at the language. He transferred a couple of cryptanalysts he had trained to Hong Kong, and did not again become involved with Japanese military systems until 1942.

He would make one additional major contribution in the first years of the war to the British effort against Japanese cryptologic systems. When Britain joined the U.S. in declaring war on Japan, he and other GC&CS leaders recognized that they were faced with an acute shortage of Japanese linguists. The estimate provided by language experts was that it would take at least three years to train linguists, a period that was completely unacceptable given the time pressures at play. Tiltman believed the job could be done in much less time, acknowledging that he was not looking for capabilities in the spoken language, and that the vocabulary that needed to be mastered was limited and stereotyped. He estimated six months was all that was needed.

He got permission from his superiors to proceed, recruited a retired naval officer as an instructor, and set up classes in rooms above a gas company's showroom in Bedford, about fifteen miles from Bletchley Park. His experiment was a great success, producing numerous cryptolinguists whose skills, while by no means enabling them to converse at native-speaker level, were sufficient for the job at hand. They filled positions not only in GC&CS, but also in the Foreign Office and with the Indian government. The criticisms he received about the abilities of graduates of the course dealt with their lack of knowledge of spoken Japanese, and with the fact that they were not Far Eastern scholars, hence could not be relied on to extract subtle nuances of the language. Since the training was not intended to develop skills in either of those areas, Tiltman generally left such critiques pass without comment.

The year 1939 was, of course, momentous for more than Tiltman's successes against Japanese naval and military cryptosystems. As war broke out, the Military Section he headed expanded rapidly. By 1939 it had grown from its original four to about ten. In addition to the modest increase in strength it received with the outbreak of the Italian campaign in East Africa, 1938 had seen it gain a few more clerks and experienced operators. During the war it would grow to nearly two thousand. Tiltman recalled that by 1939 real results of efforts to increase the manpower available to GC&CS (begun in previous years) were becoming evident. One example he pointed to was a week-long general indoctrination course (in which he was one of the lecturers) set up for twenty-four scholars from Oxford and Cambridge who had been placed in reserve status, ready to be called to duty when needed. His impression was that this group included such future GC&CS stars as Alan Turing, Gordon Welchman, and Hugh Alexander (though here his memory may have failed him since Hugh Alexander was a graduate of King's and was not associated with Oxford or Cambridge).

## Return to Military Service

Tiltman himself was recalled to active military duty, with the rank of lieutenant colonel. The move was made primarily so that he would have official status in dealing with the French military cryptologic system, a group he liaised with several times before the collapse of the French military in June 1940. He was now in charge of Number 4 Intelligence School (the British, like the Americans, liked to hide their cryptologic efforts behind euphemisms) which consisted of his own Military Section, now located at GC&CS's wartime home in Bletchley Park, and a large number of traffic analysts in London.

The elements of GC&CS that supported the military, air, and naval efforts had been moved to Bletchley Park in mid-August just before the war broke out, and the rest of the organization followed shortly thereafter. Their former home in the Broadway buildings across from St. James Park Underground Station was considered both too small and too vulnerable to air attack. So, GC&CS moved to the former estate of the owner of a chain of tobacco stores, some fifty miles north of London, an area considered safe from the anticipated German air assault. Tiltman noted after the war with some sense of irony that the move actually placed GC&CS within a quarter mile of railroad marshalling yards, a prime target in the coming air war. Fortunately, Bletchley Park was bombed only once, with negligible damage, probably as a result of a German pilot jettisoning his bomb load while trying to escape British fighter aircraft.

In dealing with the large influx of new people brought on by the war, Tiltman wanted to avoid the situation he had faced at the beginning of his own cryptologic career when he had been pretty much left to his own devices to learn the business. As he described his first days at GC&CS, he was sat down, shown a cipher, and told to get to work breaking it. While that approach might work with selected individuals, especially when they enjoyed the luxury of a peacetime environment, he recognized it as a recipe for disaster if applied generally and under the pressures of wartime. So he set up a basic cryptanalysis course for new people to introduce them to the fundamentals of the trade. But he did not believe that training could go beyond enhancing skills that had to be innately present. All training could do was stimulate intelligence and imagination. In his view, cryptanalysts were born, not made.

## Relations with the French

As we have seen, Tiltman's resumption of military rank was done largely to facilitate his dealings with the French, a relationship that had begun in May 1933 when he was working the Comintern problem. He resumed his close cooperation with Bertrand, even gaining access to the areas where the French were working on Enigma. Although both the French and the British benefited from work done by the Poles, each was rather reticent about fully sharing its efforts at exploitation with the other. Bertrand continued to amaze Tiltman with his uncanny ability to foresee where a discussion was going, a trait that enabled him to head off embarrassing situations. As Tiltman recalled, Bertrand intuitively knew when he was about to be asked a question he could not answer for security reasons, and would always interrupt his interlocutor with the phrase *"ne pas demandez,"* "don't ask."

Tiltman also liked to recall another anecdote related to his dealings with Bertrand. A couple of days after the beginning of the war, a German aircraft was shot down over Edinburgh, and a map containing the German Luftwaffe grid system for the North Sea was recovered. The map eventually found its way to Bletchley Park, and was hung on the office wall of the head of the Air Section, Josh Cooper. Tiltman pointed out that Cooper had a sensitive soul, and thought that the many ladies who had to enter his office and see the map would be bothered by the blood stains on it. He consulted with a staff member who was a pathologist by training to find a way to remove the stains without damaging the grid. A method was found, and during the cleansing, Cooper invoked the following from *Macbeth*:

> **Will all great Neptune's ocean wash this blood**
> **Clean from my hand? No; this my hand will rather**
> **The multitudinous seas incarnadine,**
> **Making the green one red.**

The map was henceforth christened "Lady Macbeth" (even though the invoked passage is by Macbeth himself, not his wife).

When, in May 1940, Bertrand finally introduced Tiltman to the area where the French worked on Enigma, Tiltman responded by presenting "Lady Macbeth" to his French colleague as a souvenir. He remembered spending about twenty minutes telling the story behind it, complete with the *Macbeth* quote only to find that the story lost everything in translation. The French never could be brought to see the humor in it.

By mid-May 1940, only days after the Germans launched their offensive against the Netherlands, Belgium, and France, Bertrand was convinced that France was about to fall. He told Tiltman that, while France valued the party GC&CS had sent to France, the time had come to get them out. He further made a remarkable promise. Bertrand reassured his allies that nothing they had worked on together, particularly Enigma, would fall into German hands. Amazingly, that promise was kept, even though at least a hundred French officers knew about the work being done on Enigma. The

Germans never became aware of the extent to which the French and the British had penetrated Enigma. Bertrand was able to keep to his commitment even though he himself was picked up by the Abwehr (German military intelligence) during the war and questioned.

One of Bertrand's final acts before the French collapse fell into the category of lost opportunities. He handed to Tiltman, without explanation, a paper that contained a number of five-figure groups. The British, unaware of what it represented, filed it away. Only later, after much effort by both the British and the Americans to break into the system, did they realize that Bertrand had handed them the front page of the German diplomatic double-additive system known to the Allies as Floradora. One can only guess how much effort could have been spared had the British recognized what they were handed, or had Bertrand fully explained it to them.

In addition to his work coordinating efforts with the French, in March 1940 Tiltman was sent to Finland during the last two weeks of the Russo-Finnish War. He was not able to provide the Finns with much cryptologic help. His sole contribution was to tell them that the Soviet submarines operating in the Baltic were using one-time pads; hence, their messages were unbreakable as long as the system was used correctly, as it was. For his part, he received from the Finns a number of captured Soviet naval codebooks, copies of which would later be provided to the Americans.

## Early War Work at Bletchley Park

Tiltman's responsibilities at Bletchley Park became, and would remain throughout the war, varied. He claimed that he was never comfortable working with machine systems, and his experiences with the most famous German system, Enigma, were limited. This did not prevent him, as we shall see, from doing the extensive linguistic work that led to the British being able to break into a very sophisticated German cipher machine, the one the British called Tunny. He was, moreover, without equal in dealing with nonmachine, or hand, systems. Even before the war, he was recognized as the person to whom undiagnosed systems were handed for successful exploitation. And his successes, even on seemingly innocuous or unimportant systems, led to greater breakthroughs on the more glamorous ones, and to intelligence insights that proved not only valuable but chilling in the knowledge they provided.

For example, in 1939 and 1940 he was successful in breaking into a succession of field ciphers the German military was using for general weather forecasts. Other systems he worked on included those used by the German railway, and ones employed by the police and the SS (Schutzstaffel, the organ of the Nazi Party charged with, among other things, central security and the extermination of "undesirable elements" in society). The railway used a variant of the Enigma machine, but without some of the security devices built into the military and naval versions. The traffic derived from his break-in enabled the British to detect large troop movements to the east in 1941. This information formed part of the basis of the warnings British prime minister Churchill sent to the Soviets that they were about to be attacked. The Soviet leader, Joseph Stalin, chose to see in these warnings an imperialist-capitalist plot to draw him into a war with Germany, so he ignored them. Hundreds of thousands of Soviet troops paid the price for his ideologically driven blindness.

Insight into the SS and police systems enabled reporters to follow the matter-of-fact reports turned in on the results of actions to "cleanse" the areas in the east occupied by German troops as they rolled into the Soviet Union. They also read with increasing horror the precise reports of "discharges" from the numerous concentration camps established by the German killing machine. In one of the great incongruities of war, the section assigned to work this target had been set up in one of the rooms in the original mansion house at Bletchley Park, rather than the military huts built on the estate grounds to house the other elements at work. The room they were given had been a nursery. They read and tabulated the results of German implementation of the "Final Solution" in a room decorated with Peter Rabbit wallpaper.

Tiltman's preference for working nonmachine ciphers in no way implies an inability to work on more sophisticated systems. In addition to his work on Enigma variants noted above, he was also responsible for the initial breakthroughs against another German high-level machine. The German high command, that is, Adolf Hitler and his generals, employed teleprinter to communicate amongst themselves with messages enciphered using principally the Lorenz SZ40 cipher machine. The British came to refer to this system as Tunny. Once it was understood how Tunny was used, and by whom, it was recognized that the contents of these messages would provide a "grand strategy" complement to the knowledge contained in Enigma enciphered messages. As an undiagnosed system, the initial attack on Tunny became Tiltman's responsibility, though at this stage the full import of the system was not appreciated (and would not be until Tiltman's abilities allowed messages sent on the system to be read). By 1941 he had identified the encipherment system used (a binary additive system) and made the initial break-in, which led to what was to become a hugely valuable and productive cryptanalytic industry in GC&CS, on a par with the Enigma work.

The weakness of Tunny was caused by operator laziness. Having demonstrated that the normal international five-unit teleprinter coding was used, Tiltman next established the additive nature of the key from the short introductory depths (two separate messages sent using the same machine settings, as not infrequently happened when the machine was first introduced in 1941). If he added such messages together, the result was the intermixed stream of the two plaintexts. Operators usually recognized their error and stopped such depths after at most a few dozen letters. In late August 1941, however, a German operator sent a long message and was then asked to repeat it. In an amazing mistake, he did this using the same cipher settings but retyped the whole message. Within a few characters from the start his second transmission (with varying abbreviations and errors) diverged from his first, producing not only a long depth but one with basically the same underlying plaintext in both parts.

The two transmissions still contained various garbles, and the recovery of the plaintexts (and hence the corresponding key) took Tiltman some time. Thereafter his Research Section, and particularly William Tutte, who made the first break-in, solved the Lorenz machine early in 1942. Machine setups were different on different links, and the various elements of the machine (it involved twelve pinwheels with a total of 501 pins, and various later complications) were changed with ever-increasing frequency. By 1943 GC&CS realized that large-scale mechanization was both necessary and feasible, which led to the first practical application of a large-scale program-controlled computer named Colossus to exploit it. By the end of the war, ten of these machines were in use.

Something of the intellectual accomplishment breaking into the Tunny system represented (and Tiltman's self-effacing wit) can be seen by an anecdote Tiltman recalled years after the war. Shortly after the end of the conflict, two Tunny machines captured from Field Marshal Kesselring's (the commander of German forces in Italy) train arrived at Bletchley, and Tiltman was asked to explain how he had broken into the system in the first place. He replied that he was able to use the twelve-letter indicator of each message. When it was pointed out to him that the captured machines had no letters on them, he replied, "I can't help that, this is the first time I've seen it too."

Ironically, shortly after the August 1941 messages were sent, the Germans made improvements to their use of the system, and never again was key from depths resolvable on a sufficient scale to have recovered the whole machine. Without those two messages, and Tiltman's adept exploitation of them, the British would not have been able to break into Tunny. To gain some idea of the value of his breakthrough, in March 1945 alone Tunny transmissions totaling some five million characters, containing intelligence of critical importance, were deciphered. As an additional indication of the importance GC&CS placed on Tunny exploitation, by 1944 some 500 people were involved in cryptanalytic efforts against this system, with another 600 involved in intercept and processing of Tunny traffic.

Tiltman would later point to the exploitation of Tunny as a case of pure cryptanalytic work. GC&CS regularly received captured (or stolen) codebooks or cipher keys on other systems, but for Tunny none was ever forthcoming. He pointed to GC&CS success here to counter postwar claims that cryptographic systems were not broken by pure cryptanalytic effort, but always relied on captured machines, codebooks, or cipher keys.

## Work Habits/Personality

By this time Tiltman had developed his work habits as well as certain axioms that framed his efforts through the war and beyond. He found that most of his useful thinking went on at a level just below full consciousness. Success came when he was able to so immerse himself in a system that the solution would be formulated quite subconsciously. Because of that, he preferred to do his own preliminary analysis, registration, and indexing, disdaining the use of machines except for simple sorting and listing. A true indication of his genius was that he relied on intuition born of experience to tell when a tenuous lead had played out and needed to be abandoned. Since he firmly believed that cryptanalysis in the diagnostic stage was more an art than a science, he warned against fear of making mistakes (remember that he was amused with, not embarrassed by, his Chinese Telegraphic Code experience). Paths that turned out to be blind were learning experiences, not failures.

He had a clear understanding of his own limitations. He admitted to having no knowledge of higher mathematics (something not considered a drawback in prewar Britain--most of the cryptanalysts hired before the war were anything but mathematicians), and claimed only an instinctive grasp of probability theory. In addition, as we have seen earlier, he denied being a linguist, though he would eventually break codes and ciphers in over a dozen languages (languages whose roots varied from Indo-European to Asiatic to Semitic). He insisted, however, that a research cryptanalyst needed a working knowledge of comparative linguistics and an ear for the sound patterns of unfamiliar languages. And, as we have also seen, he placed great stock on cryptanalysts gaining a general working knowledge of the other branches of SIGINT, much as he had done while serving at Simla.

One of the peculiarities about Tiltman noticed by his associates was that he never worked sitting down. Rather, he had a desk specially constructed that allowed him to stand while puzzling over the latest cipher system to come to his attention. He also demonstrated a singular ability to concentrate on the problem at hand, and then to essentially forget all about it once he had done his part and had moved on to another issue. One of his wartime colleagues remembered in particular passing him a system which had stumped several analysts for a number of weeks. Tiltman unraveled it in two days. When approached a few weeks later and updated on further progress made against it, he had completely forgotten about it and had to be reminded of the salient points.

He surprised many with his lack of concern for the mundane protocols of military life, this in spite of the fact that he remained, throughout his life, most military in bearing himself. Upon being recalled to active service in 1939, he readily admitted that he could no longer remember whether his insignia of rank should be mounted above or below the crown on his uniform. He repeatedly drove his adjutant at Bletchley Park, a major consumed with enforcing proper military bearing and decorum, to distraction with his informal practices such as granting weekend passes to subordinates who merely knocked on his door and asked, bypassing the adjutant completely.

Tiltman rarely wore his own uniform, and instituted changes in the uniforms of others. For instance, when William Filby (later a renowned cryptanalyst in his own right, but at the time a newly minted private) first reported for duty in 1940, he marched up to

Tiltman's desk, halted in the time-honored fashion of the British army with a vigorous stomp of his boots, and saluted. Tiltman looked at Filby's feet, and exclaimed, "I say, old boy, need you wear those things?" referring to Filby's army issue boots. From that day forward, Filby added white sneakers to his regulation uniform. Needless to say, the shoes, plus Tiltman's incurable habit of referring to an enlisted subordinate as "old boy," did nothing to endear him to military perfectionists.

In another example, Tiltman, as a senior officer, had to deal with his own chauffeur who had "borrowed" Tiltman's official vehicle for a tryst with his girlfriend, and then had the misfortune of crashing the vehicle. Tiltman's inclination to deal with the matter quietly and personally had to give way to military propriety, and he was forced to convene and preside over a court-martial, his first. Again, he frustrated his adjutant, and provided mirth for everyone else involved, by constantly asking the major what he was supposed to do next during the proceedings, and by asking the accused if what was happening met with his approval.

He showed his human side in many other ways throughout the war. He intervened personally when necessary to make sure members of his section were paid properly and on time. He went so far as to get money advanced to individuals when the army pay system broke down, as it is wont to do in the British Army as in any other. On another occasion, he took the time to intervene directly to make sure that promises made to commission graduates of his Japanese training course when they went to India were kept. The time taken out of his hectic schedule to follow-up until the commissions were all granted he considered a small price to pay to ensure proper treatment of his people.

His willingness to be flexible in the matter of uniform use did not stem from any disdain for military practices. Instead, it was an acknowledgement that the war had caused a truly odd assortment of individuals to be called to the colors and assembled at Bletchley Park. He never lost sight of the goal, which was to gather the best minds available to break Axis ciphers. All other matters were secondary, and should not be allowed to get in the way of getting the job done.

That the people doing the job, or being prepared to do the job, were of the utmost importance to him was clearly shown by the emphasis he placed on ensuring proper training which extended, as noted, to both language preparation and making sure that each new cryptanalyst received a firm grounding in the business they were now about. His involvement did not end with the establishment of the schools to provide the necessary training. He would often take time from a frenetic wartime schedule to visit the classes and talk to the students to inquire about their progress. His ability to impart his skills to the young and to inspire their enthusiasm and success continued until he was in his eighties. He is said to have made the difficult appear easy and the seemingly impossible seem a worthwhile challenge.

## Initial Relations with the U.S.

Interestingly enough, it was most likely precisely Tiltman's ability to put formalistic trappings aside that enabled him to make his greatest contribution not only to the war effort, but to the postwar cryptologic world as well, the cementing of relations between the United States and Great Britain in the arena of signals intelligence and communications security. The Americans saw him as the embodiment of British eccentric brilliance, a perceived stereotype the Americans have always found endearing. At the same time, he avoided the perception of falling into the negative American stereotype of the British, that of officious condescension. He reciprocated their warm acceptance, and added a toleration of U.S. habits not generally found among his colleagues. A truly close personal and official relationship blossomed essentially from initial contact.

That first encounter came even before U.S. entry into the war. As early as 1940, British prime minister Winston Churchill recognized that U.S. entry into the war on the side of Britain was essential to success, and instructed his naval and military forces, and his intelligence services, to prepare for full cooperation with their American counterparts. These instructions perfectly complemented the thinking of U.S. president Franklin Roosevelt, who also understood that only by the U.S. standing together with Britain could German and Japanese aggression be defeated.

With this atmosphere set at the highest levels, exchanges of visits at a variety of levels dealing with numerous topics began. On the SIGINT side, a four-person American delegation (consisting of Major Abraham Sinkov and Captain Leo Rosen for the Army, and Lieutenants Robert Weeks and Prescott Currier for the Navy) visited Bletchley Park in early 1941. The four traveled to Britain aboard the British battleship HMS *King George V* escorting a beef convoy that had originated in South America and then to the naval base at Scapa Flow, Scotland, and hence by cruiser, HMS *Neptune*, to England. They carried with them information on U.S.

cryptologic work against the Japanese, to include an analog of the Japanese diplomatic machine the Americans called Purple.

The trip, especially the final leg, was not without incident. The original plan called for the group to be met at Scapa Flow by a representative from the U.S. embassy with two flying boats to transport them and their equipment to the south of England. They had, however, brought some thirty crates of material weighing up to two tons. Some of the crates were too large to fit through the hatch of the flying boats, so that option could not be used. The captain of HMS *King George V* then arranged with an acquaintance who commanded HMS *Neptune* to give the Americans a ride south. While in the Channel, the ship was spotted by German aerial reconnaissance and attacked by two German dive-bombers. While none of the personnel on board were wounded, the crates of equipment, tied down on deck, were all hit by machine gun fire as the bombers strafed the ship. At this point the luck of war intervened, and the would-be Allies benefited from the fact that the Germans had chosen to ignore the provisions of the Geneva Convention on armaments by using explosive rounds in their machine guns. As a result, the rounds exploded on contact with the crates rather than penetrating them. The equipment the Americans were bringing to demonstrate to the British escaped damage.

The British, especially Tiltman, were impressed by the willingness of the Americans to share their most sensitive cryptologic successes. In particular, Tiltman thought that in turning over the Purple analog the Americans had made what he called "a magnificent gesture," one that bound the British to in turn share their closely held successes against the German Enigma machine. Tiltman ran into no opposition in turning over what he knew about Japanese military systems, most of which was new to the Americans, who had been concentrating on Japanese diplomatic and naval systems.

His superiors, particularly A. G. Denniston, were caught off guard by the openness of their soon-to-be allies, and there appears to have been considerable debate about what full disclosure meant. They especially wanted to withhold information on the successes Britain had achieved in tackling the Enigma machine. They had concerns about American security practices (which, given the notorious weakness of U.S. codes and ciphers up to this time, were not unwarranted), and feared that the Americans would inadvertently reveal information that the Germans could use to identify and correct their own cryptologic vulnerabilities. Since Britain was dependent on continued success against the naval Enigma in particular for survival, they did not think their concerns were unreasonable.

British sensitivities about the security of Enigma ran deep, and extended throughout those in the know in British governmental and military establishments. When the first successes against the system had been achieved, attempts were made to disguise the source by attributing all the intelligence to a spy codenamed Boniface, but that fiction soon wore thin. What the Boniface myth gave them, as Tiltman later described it, was a system that divided recipients of the material into three groups. The first set was fully in the know. The second was not, and its members were "too dumb" to figure out the truth. As a result, their distrust of material provided by spies led them to disregard the intelligence altogether. The third group was potentially the most dangerous. Its members were not in the know, but had figured it out. Since they had not been briefed, no restrictions were placed on whatever speculation they chose to indulge in. They did, however, accept the intelligence and used it to great effect. Given that the British had devised this elaborate scheme for handling Enigma material within their own ranks, their reluctance to be forthcoming with the Americans becomes more understandable.

Tiltman, perhaps in small part because he was not as attached to the Enigma problem, but very largely due to his judgment of what was at stake, took a broader view of the issue. Given American openness with Purple, he believed that British reticence over Enigma would be nothing but a cause for future trouble since it made a mockery of the entire concept of full exchange of information. He argued that the American delegation could not help but notice that they were being denied access to large sections of Bletchley Park. They would inevitably draw conclusions from that fact, which would not be in the best interests of furthering relations between themselves and GC&CS.

He took his case over Denniston's head to Sir Stewart Menzies, "C," who as well as being head of the British Secret Intelligence Service (SIS, popularly known as "MI 6") was also administratively responsible for GC&CS. After considerable discussion, Menzies conceded that sharing was necessary, but insisted on stringent preconditions. The American delegation would have to provide the British with a list of the names of individuals they intended to share the information with, and agree to not add anyone to the list without prior British permission. And this agreement was to be made in writing *before* even the scope of the British Enigma effort was revealed to them. It was very much the cryptologic equivalent of buying a pig in a poke.

The Americans, junior officers all, not unnaturally balked at the very thought of signing such a commitment, no doubt envisioning the repercussions that would follow when they returned home. They saw in the preconditions the very embodiment of the officious condescension Americans had almost by instinct historically associated with the British. Their fury was probably exceeded only by the degree to which the responsibility they were being asked to assume appalled them. Tiltman again used all his powers of persuasion, this time with the Americans, to convince them, sight unseen, that the prize was worth the game, and they finally signed. His success laid the foundation for unparalleled cooperation that continues to this day. The preconditions, and continued British reticence with regards to Enigma, left bad feelings that Tiltman continued to have to deal with.

The cryptologic services of the soon-to-be allies continued to cement their budding relationship in the fall of 1941. In September Tiltman worked with Denniston to arrange for Geoffrey Stevens, one of the men he had trained and sent to Hong Kong (the unit he served with had since been moved to Singapore), to be posted to Washington. Stevens became the first regular liaison between GC&CS and its American counterparts.

With the entry of the U.S. into the war in December 1941, cooperation between the cryptologic services of the two countries deepened. By spring 1942, it was the turn of the British to cross the Atlantic, and who better to represent GC&CS than the one individual who had almost single-handedly saved the nascent relationship in 1941. Tiltman boarded a U.S. warship, laden with eight heavy mailbags filled with reports and technical information from Bletchley Park. The crossing was not without its moments of levity, at least in retrospect. He recalled later that his instructions were to keep the bags in his cabin at all times (given the size of accommodations on warships, that alone must have presented some degree of discomfort), but he was to move them to the side of the ship for removal or sinking in case of emergency. Since he was barely able to lift even one of the bags, he had to prevail on the good graces of his hosts to let him know in advance when drills would be held (so he would not have to move the material needlessly), and to detail a party of seamen to assist in moving the bags in the event of a real emergency. Fortunately, none arose.

During the voyage he was made party to what amounted to a breach of security by the communications officer of the ship. Knowing something of Tiltman's mission (the officer handled enciphered messages), he took it upon himself to show Tiltman the secure communications gear he was responsible for. Tiltman promised himself to cover the officer's well-intentioned indiscretion by acting as if he had never seen the gear when he would be shown it officially. Upon his arrival in the U.S., both the Navy (in the person of Joseph Wenger) and the Army (through William Friedman) demonstrated the gear for him, each independently of the other. As it turned out, Wenger had received authorization for his actions. Friedman, much like the naval officer aboard ship, discussed the equipment on his own authority. This, according to Tiltman, led to a confrontation between Friedman and General Strong, the staff intelligence officer (G-2) for General Marshall, which may have led to one of Friedman's breakdowns.

The material and expertise that Tiltman brought with him would prove to be invaluable to the Americans. Included were Vichy French colonial codebooks complete with cryptanalytic notes and comments by GC&CS's French section, microfilms of materials related to British efforts to exploit the German diplomatic Floradora system, and information from the GC&CS Research Section (which Tiltman had set up) on the methods they used to solve several complex ciphers. The methods involved were unknown to the Americans, who quickly put these new insights to work.

Tiltman's instructions for his visit (which lasted a month from late March to late April 1942) included working out a full interchange of information with the U.S. cryptologic efforts, and to see if he could do anything to encourage the Army and Navy to be more cooperative amongst themselves. He quickly realized that trying to insert himself into the peculiar tribal rituals which made up Army-Navy relations would only be counterproductive, and he backed away, ignoring that part of his instructions. He was also to try to effect GC&CS's desired division of effort with the Americans whereby the U.S. would concentrate its efforts against Japanese systems, leaving German and Italian ones to the UK. Enigma continued to be a *bête-noire*, with many in the upper reaches of GC&CS (particularly Commander Travis, who had just effectively replaced Denniston as head of GC&CS) still reluctant to fully share technical information with the U.S. Travis was especially loath to have the Americans spend resources duplicating the British effort.

For his part, Tiltman was impressed by the efforts being made in the Navy's OP-20-G office against Japanese naval systems, especially JN-25. He professed to being staggered by the number of tabulating machines in use (remember, his preference was still, and would remain throughout his career, to work by hand). He was not totally won over to this "automated" way of attacking cipher systems.

The U.S. was willing to accept that part of the proposed division of effort which pertained to Japanese systems. The Army's Signals Intelligence Service (predecessor of the Army Security Agency, which was later to become part of the Intelligence and Security Command

(INSCOM)) in particular was reluctant to develop a formal working agreement, but tight resources created such an arrangement by default. Tiltman had been authorized to limit U.S. access to traffic and cryptanalytic material should such a step prove necessary. He recognized innately that any attempt at such heavy-handed tactics would produce results the opposite of those desired, so he wisely held his hand in this matter.

Where the Americans had considerable difficulty accepting the British proposal came with Enigma, particularly the system used by U-boats which had converted to a four-wheel machine on 1 February 1942 and which the British, at the time, could not read. With U.S. merchant shipping losses in the North Atlantic and along the U.S. coast mounting, it was difficult for the U.S. Navy to accept the British position that they were best equipped to deal with the problem on their own. The U.S. wanted a copy of the British bombe (the machine being used to break into Enigma keys based on cribs), and they wanted to develop their own versions of that machine. To make any such effort worthwhile, however, they would be dependent on receiving German intercepted traffic from the British since the U.S., at the time, had precious little in the way of collection resources in the European theater of operations.

The American officer who put considerable pressure on the British was Rear Admiral Joseph Redman, director of naval communications, and he singled Tiltman out for attack. Tiltman again used all his persuasive powers to break down the reluctance of his boss, this time Commander Travis. By mid-May 1942, he had succeeded to the point where GC&CS was willing to admit to the Americans the reasons for its difficulties in dealing with the four-wheel Enigma. A further concession was an agreement to allow the Americans to study the British bombe, and Travis promised to provide one at, the Americans understood, the earliest possible moment (which, given the few machines in existence, and the need for all of them to be operational, did not promise to be in the immediate future, especially since Travis intended the timeframe to be August-September). Because of that, and the natural misunderstandings that arose out of varied interpretations of "earliest possible moment," Enigma continued to plague U.S.-UK relations.

Tiltman himself was not immune to the problems the Enigma matter caused. In fact, it was responsible for some of the more unpleasant incidents of his visit. We have already seen that Admiral Redman zeroed in on him. In addition, he had asked at one point for a meeting with Agnes Driscoll, the formidable Navy cryptanalyst, to hear her ideas about Enigma. He went unsuspecting to the meeting, which turned out to be on the stage of an auditorium in front of an audience of technical experts from both services. He recalled that this included Friedman, Rowlett, Sinkov, Kullback, and the heads of both the Army and Navy cryptologic services. Mrs. Driscoll then proceeded to grill him on the British effort against Enigma, a subject he willingly admitted he was ill equipped to deal with, given that he had barely ever worked on the machine. She was convinced that the British were making more to-do about the solution to Enigma than was necessary, and she claimed to be able to do the job properly. She believed, however, that the British were withholding a vital piece of information, and that their refusal to share it was all that was thwarting the U.S. effort. She was wrong on both counts, but Tiltman was in no position to argue the point because of his technical ignorance of the subject. Decades later he still ruefully remembered the experience.

The visit to the U.S. had a lighter side as well. During a meeting with Friedman, while the latter was going over some of the reports that Tiltman had brought with him from GC&CS, he looked up from his reading and asked what a "finnery" was. Tiltman indicated that he did not know for sure, but believed it must refer to a practice the Finns had of changing the key settings on their Hagelin machines in mid-message. Friedman was satisfied with this, and began using the term as part of his cryptologic jargon. The punch line came only after Tiltman returned to Bletchley Park. He called in his assistant and asked why he had not been briefed on "finnery." The assistant had to somewhat sheepishly explain that there was no such thing. The term had gotten into a message as a result of a cryptographic bust and had not been caught in the editing process.

All in all, the trip was a success. Enigma, however, remained a sticking point (and Tiltman's relationship with Admiral Redman was destined to get worse), and would continue to cause problems, as we shall see. He could not prevent efforts by the Americans to begin building their own bombes, especially to deal with the four-rotor machine introduced by the German submarine service, an area where the version developed by the U.S. Navy would prove superior to the British ones. But that was essentially the only major point of contention between the new allies. Agreement was reached on the U.S. taking primacy in dealing with Japanese systems. Tiltman made arrangements for British intercept of Japanese communications to be routed to Washington for American processing. He also made arrangements for the Navy to send two or three officers to GC&CS to study how the British had set up research groups so that the naval effort to set up similar groups would not have to relearn lessons the British had mastered.

The naval officers were but the vanguard of a much larger American contingent. By the summer of 1942 the first of what were to be over 100 U.S. Army personnel arrived at Bletchley, eventually headed by William Bundy, the future foreign policy advisor to both Presidents Kennedy and Johnson and coauthor of the Tonkin Gulf Resolution. Tiltman considered this one of the noblest gestures of the war, and readily admitted that the influx of American manpower, here as in other aspects of the joint endeavor, made a critical difference. The flow of personnel the other way was not as great, necessarily so given the relative numbers involved. Tiltman's contribution from the British perspective was to make sure that the British contingent to the U.S. remained a unit under British control. Commander Travis had been inclined to turn complete control over to the Americans, but Tiltman intervened, arguing that this would risk fragmenting the British contingent and dissipating its influence.

In addition to building relationships with the Americans, Tiltman also used this visit (as he would use each visit to this side of the "pond") to strengthen cryptanalytic relations with Canada. He retained interesting memories of Canada. He noted that there always seemed to be a layer of bureaucracy missing in the way Canadians handled things. As he put it, you would run into an obscure Signals officer who would just happen to have a close friend who just happened to be chief of the general staff, and neither of the friends would see anything wrong with using that connection to get things done. The lack of the red tape more commonly associated with both the British and Americans was refreshing.

Tiltman returned to Britain, but not uneventfully. He flew back in an unheated Liberator bomber that developed problems as it approached Scotland and had to execute a crash landing at Prestwick airport at full speed with flaps down in an attempt, successful as it turned out, to bring the plane to a safe stop. He had cemented the high regard Americans held him in by bringing them codebooks, cipher tables, and the benefit of his own professional observations on a range of cryptanalytic problems. That he returned essentially empty-handed was a suggestion of the true state of the relationship between the allies in the first half of 1942. The UK was still well out in front of the U.S., and the British had to content themselves with intangible contributions from the Americans that came in the form of discussions, observations, and insights.

## COMSEC Efforts

Back at Bletchley, nonliaison tasks awaited Tiltman's attention. Before his trip to the U.S., he had been named to replace "Dilly" Knox as GC&CS Chief Cryptographer. Interestingly, Tiltman always recollected that he had replaced Oliver Strachey in this role. Strachey had, in fact, been replaced by Knox in 1939, with Tiltman replacing Knox in 1942. Tiltman and Knox never got on with each other, so it may not be surprising that this should prove to one of the rare times when Tiltman's memory betrayed him. On numerous occasions he admitted that he never understood how Knox had achieved the reputation that he had. Tiltman's recollections of his dealings with Knox mostly involved the end of Knox's career, at a time when he was terminally ill, so that may account for his less than favorable opinion. Tiltman also acknowledged that, at one of his first meetings with Knox, he committed the tactless and (for a cryptanalyst) unforgivable sin of reading a stretch of key Knox had recovered over his shoulder and rendering it into English. This ranks right up among the social graces alongside of someone who looks over your shoulder while you are completing a crossword puzzle and provides you with the answers before you have time to fill them in yourself.

Tiltman would later claim that the title of Chief Cryptographer was largely an honorary one, meaning he received no extra compensation for it. In fact he was amused to learn after the war from a captured German that his foes thought that the British Chief Cryptographer was paid more than the Archbishop of Canterbury. In reality the position carried several tangible responsibilities. His duties included taking over or giving advice on the attack on any undiagnosed or unexploited system, a role he had been filling in any case given his reputation for dealing with such systems. A second part of the job was to oversee the development of secure British ciphers. For this later task he was given a twelve-man staff, and with those limited resources he was expected to advise on the technical security of military, naval, diplomatic, and other cipher systems. He estimated that he spent about one-fifth of his time during the war designing cipher systems to replace ones which had been shown to be inadequate for the conditions under which they had to be used.

His most significant personal contribution to this effort eventually (from late 1943) helped to secure British naval communications for the rest of the war. The cipher system the Royal Navy had been using had become vulnerable both because of German skill in attacking it, and because it was being overused. Britain had developed a very good rotor machine called Typex (a variant of the commercial Enigma machine), but could never produce enough of them to service all the users who had to have secure communications. This left the British dependent on hand-made systems which, by nature, were subject to overuse. While all branches of the British armed forces faced this problem, it was especially critical for the Royal Navy. Its system was used by the American, British, and Canadian navies up to mid-1943; 1,700 holders, all of whom had to be in a position to communicate securely, were dependent on what was a vulnerable system. The fact that three allied navies needed to communicate jointly only compounded the problem of overuse and the criticality of coming up with a solution.

Tiltman replaced it with a system he designed. The refinement he introduced consisted of a plastic grille which contained 100 four-digit-wide windows randomly spaced. This was superimposed over an additive sheet that had forty-eight lines of sixty-eight digits each. Setting squares for the placement of the grille provided 100 possible settings, and a conversion table appeared on each sheet with mixed sequences of digits from 00 to 99 for indicating purposes. Each sheet was used for one day only. The placement of the grille was determined through a substitution pattern sent to each user. This fulfilled one of Tiltman's basic prerequisites for the security of any cipher system. Security had to be taken entirely out of the hands of the users; otherwise, they would create shortcuts that would destroy any semblance of protection.

Known as the Stencil Subtractor Frame (S.S. Frame or SSF), it was put into fleet-wide use in December 1943. Combined with the introduction of a new codebook in June 1943, it fixed the problems the Royal Navy had been experiencing, and German ability to exploit its communications ceased effectively from June. Their recoveries of the new codebook were ended by the introduction of the SSF. They were able, through an impressive piece of cryptanalytic research, to diagnose how the SSF worked through attacking a month's worth of auxiliary ship traffic and by throwing large numbers of analysts against the problem, but this diagnostic success only served to convince them that they would be unable to exploit the system. The Germans had used their ability to read the British naval system to great effect in attacking convoys coming from America and Canada. That effectiveness had already begun to disappear by May 1943 when improved convoy methods forced the Germans to withdraw their submarines from the North Atlantic. The introduction of new codebooks, first in June 1943, then, as we have seen, in conjunction with the S.S. Frame in late 1943, put paid to any thoughts the Germans might have entertained of regaining that advantage. While Tiltman's contribution was by no means the sole, or even the principal, cause for the German defeat, it certainly played a role. The

British government recognized the value of his effort by awarding him 1,000 pounds in 1944 for the invention of this cipher device, orders for which had by then reached over 17,000.

A second system introduced by Tiltman enjoyed less success, at least as far as the Allies were concerned. This was the Cysquare, loosely based on a grille system he had developed while serving in India in the 1920s. As mentioned earlier, he had believed that system to be secure, but his own subsequent study of it showed him its weaknesses, which he promptly remedied. He had also worked on improving it throughout the 1930s, a period when his activities were actually frowned on since it was thought that cryptanalysts should not waste their time developing ciphers or ciphering systems. Faced with the need for a low-echelon cipher system, he developed Cysquare for use by the British Eighth Army in North Africa. It was a resounding failure. Operators soon found out that desert conditions made it impossible to distinguish between the cells they were supposed to use and the ones that were "grayed" out. They rapidly abandoned it for other methods.

Interestingly, Tiltman's system was not dismissed as readily by his enemies. The Germans captured a number of the stencils during the North African campaign and thought the concept had considerable merit. They modified it and used it as one source (there were others, to be sure) to create their own field cipher, known as Rasterschlüssel, which came into wide use in October 1944. Tiltman noted ruefully that the British had considerable trouble with this system. He believed they would not have been able to break into it had the Germans not made mistakes while producing the pads required for its use.

## Japanese Attaché System

In 1942 Tiltman once again took up his efforts against Japanese systems, this time turning his attention to the cipher used by the Japanese military attachés. The problem had originally been assigned to a number of French cryptanalysts who had managed to escape after the collapse of the French Army in 1940, and were now working at Bletchley Park. By early 1942, Tiltman was not at all pleased with the progress (or lack thereof) the French were making, and he opted to take over the effort personally. He soon found that the French had completely misdiagnosed the cipher, believing it to be a combined substitution and transposition system.

Tiltman quickly corrected the misdiagnosis, and discovered that he was dealing with a digraph code in which there were digraphs for basic kana symbols and for words and phrases commonly used in military communications. The two-letter groups were then set in a square grid in adjacent squares in either a horizontal or diagonal pattern and read vertically to form the encoded text. This was then enciphered using a "literal additive," adding letters rather than numbers.

As is often the case, Tiltman's exploitation of the system was aided by mistakes by Japanese code clerks and by the stereotyped nature of the communications he was dealing with. The code clerks helped by making the classic mistake code clerks have made for as long as there have been code clerks. They kept reusing portions of the additive table (often out of sheer necessity, they had more messages to send than their keying system would support), providing their enemies with depth. The attachés themselves provided assistance as well through their formalistic phraseology. Each message began with the pat phrase "I have the honor to report to your excellency that..." With that generous crib as an aid, Tiltman was soon able to strip away the mystery of the system, baring the secrets contained within it.

To exploit that crib, however, Tiltman had to rely on a lesson he had learned in the 1930s about Japanese methods of encrypting their messages. In an attempt to foil attempts to exploit stereotypical beginnings, the Japanese used bisection. That is, they broke their messages into sections (sometimes as many as four), and then rearranged the order of the sections so that the beginning would fall in the middle of the transmitted text. Tiltman had learned early on to look in the interior of a Japanese message for stereotypical giveaways.

The secrets revealed by Tiltman's breakthrough proved themselves to be well worth the effort put into breaking the cipher. Throughout 1943 and 1944, the Japanese diplomatic mission in Berlin was made privy to German planning for confronting the long-anticipated Allied invasion of France. This included tours of and detailed briefings on the beach defenses the Germans were preparing, as well as insight into where the Germans expected the blow to fall. The Japanese attaché prepared meticulous reports containing this information for Tokyo, reports that were read in Washington and London with, one might expect, far more interest and concern for detail than they received from their intended recipients. They reinforced similar messages sent by the Japanese ambassador to Berlin, messages that were also read by the Allies thanks to the ability to read the Japanese diplomatic cipher system known as Purple.

Together, these two sources of information (combined with material exploited from Tunny) helped the Western Allies to prepare countermeasures for the beach defenses put in place by the Germans. More importantly, they reassured the Allies that the German high command expected that the main invasion would occur at the Pas de Calais, the narrowest part of the English Channel, and the point that would place the invaders closest to Germany's industrial heartland in the Ruhr Valley. The Allies learned that the Germans expected a landing attempt in Normandy, but believed it would be only a diversion. Allied masters of deception put their best efforts into reinforcing the German preference for a landing at the Pas de Calais. They were gratified to see their efforts paying off through their continued insight into the reports from the Japanese attaché and ambassador.

Having done the hard part, Tiltman set up a small subsection at Bletchley as part of his Military Section to handle continued exploitation of the attaché cipher. The subsection consisted of a team to handle the code and cipher breaking, plus a team to analyze the results. Tiltman had the added satisfaction of manning the subsection with graduates of the Japanese course he had established at Bedford at the beginning of the war with Japan, the effort the language "experts" had told him was doomed to failure.

## Back to the U.S./The Turing Incident

By late 1942, Tiltman was on his way back to the United States for another series of meetings. This visit would call forth every bit of ally-building skills he had to overcome a wealth of contentious issues, most centering on continued mistrust over Enigma. The announced purpose of the visit was to work out the details of field cryptographic systems to be used in joint operations. It soon turned to issues of more import to the future well-being of the cryptologic allies.

Tiltman arrived back in the U.S. in December 1942, heading a three-man team. As noted, their brief was to help implement an agreement that would allow the two countries to jointly grade their own codes and ciphers on the basis of the level of security that was needed in a given situation and that could be expected from a given system. This would, hopefully, lay the groundwork for deciding which systems could be used in joint operations where rapid accessibility to each other's communications could be vital.

At issue was that the British were, as we have seen, by and large dependent on hand systems at a tactical level. The Americans, on the other hand, had adopted the Hagelin C-38 (M-209), and wanted the British to accept that system as well. The British believed that to replace their systems with the M-209 would involve more than getting the new materials to everyone who needed them. This was a monumental task in its own right given that British forces, like their American counterparts, were deployed across the globe. It would also involve a Herculean effort to retrain British code clerks, and this in the middle of a war. In addition, the British had legitimate concerns about the security provided by the M-209. It was particularly vulnerable when overused, as it often was in the heat of combat, and both the Germans and the Japanese would prove capable of exploiting it.

As Tiltman had anticipated, the initial meetings on this subject did not go smoothly. His task was rendered more difficult because one member of the British delegation (from the Royal Air Force) adopted a confrontational attitude, even though his marching order from Tiltman for the meeting was "to keep his mouth shut." This led to the perception that there was no agreement within the British contingent, let alone between the British and the Americans. The U.S. was quick to pick up on the perceived disagreement amongst the British, and equally quick to try to exploit it. It took considerable skill on Tiltman's part to enforce discipline within his own "ranks" while continuing a dialogue with the Americans that would not put previous efforts for unity at risk over this single issue.

An agreement was finally reached, despite continued vocal opposition from the Royal Air Force representative. He objected particularly to American insistence on use of the M-209 cipher system. He had to be convinced that the U.S. was pushing for its use in part because there were 200,000 of them lying about unused. (Actually, there were only 100,000 of them, but Tiltman used the higher figure, perhaps for dramatic effect.) It was eventually agreed that the British would continue working to develop a frequently changing digraphic code, and that the M-209 would be held in reserve should the British be unable to deliver. Tiltman found an ally in William Friedman, and together they agreed that in the future codes and ciphers would be developed jointly, thereby alleviating the need to retroactively patch together a fit for incompatible systems.

The real test of his skills, however, had nothing to do with the delegation he led, or the subject they were sent to deal with. Separate from Tiltman's visit, Alan Turing, the brilliant British mathematician who was responsible for British development of the bombe, among other contributions, arrived in the U.S. His visit arose from an invitation from the U.S. Army chief signal officer to the British to send over an expert to see a new piece of equipment that was being developed for speech privacy (this would become the SIGSALY system). While Turing was en route, General Strong, the intelligence officer (G-2) for the chief of staff, General Marshall, blocked Turing's proposed visit to Bell Laboratories, where the system was being developed.

Several reasons have been advanced for General Strong's action. One involved a member of Strong's staff, another general who had ties to ITT, the company working with U.S. cryptographers to develop SIGSALY. Tiltman maintained that he was told by Carter Clarke, then chief of the Special Branch of the U.S. Army's Military Intelligence Division, after the incident was finally resolved, that this general, misinterpreting what was meant by "exploitation," persuaded Strong to block Turing's visit. The general believed that commercial exploitation was at issue, and that the British would use their access to threaten ITT's business interests once the war was over. Tiltman could not vouch for the accuracy of this explanation; he merely offered it as what he had been told by a person he respected.

Probably closer to the truth, based on the negotiations that finally broke the impasse, was that Enigma had once again reared its divisive head. The U.S. Army remained convinced that the British were withholding information from them, information that would have enabled the Americans to better pursue their own desire to exploit the German encryption machine. Apparently, the Americans saw the British request for Turing's access to SIGSALY as a wedge they could use to force the British to be more forthcoming with Enigma technical information and raw traffic intercept. It should be noted that the U.S., at this stage of the war, was entirely dependent on British collection efforts against the European Axis. Whatever Enigma intercepts there were that interested the Army came from the British because the Americans had no collection sites in a position to pick up German messages.

Whatever the cause for the dispute, Tiltman received orders to intervene with his American contacts to resolve the issue. In fact, he was told not to return to the UK until he had achieved a successful resolution. At first he met with reluctance on the part of Strong to even discuss Turing's visit. Several long meetings were held in which Strong skillfully kept the Turing topic off the agenda. In each case, Tiltman had been accompanied by British naval captain Hastings, whose job was to represent both the SIS and GC&CS with the Americans. Tiltman was then informed by Brigadier Dykes, staff officer to Field Marshal Sir John Dill, the senior British representative in Washington, that Hastings was, in fact, part of the problem. According to Dykes, Strong did not like Hastings, and would not discuss the Turing visit while he was present. Accordingly, Tiltman prevailed on Hastings to bow out, and he met with Strong by himself. As he later recalled, this did not significantly improve matters at first. Instead, he was treated to another two hours of the general covering every subject imaginable, except the Turing visit. In the middle of this, Strong stopped, and said "I know you think that I have horns and cloven hooves," which left Tiltman wondering whether the proper response was "Yes, Sir!" or "No, Sir!"

Tiltman also faced the added complication of a deadline that was caused by the impending Casablanca Conference. Since virtually everyone who could work to break the impasse would be leaving Washington for the conference, Tiltman had to move quickly. Throughout mid- to late December, Tiltman continued to meet with U.S. officials, especially Clarke and then, in January 1943, again with Strong himself to convince them that no Enigma information that could endanger American lives or operations was being withheld. By early January he was able to convince Strong of that fact, but then faced opposition from Britain. He recommended that the U.S. be allowed to send permanent representatives to Bletchley Park who would have full access to every aspect of Enigma exploitation so that the Americans would have no cause to express similar doubts about British cooperation in the future.

It finally took a direct exchange of letters between Field Marshal Sir John Dill, the former chief of the Imperial General Staff and, in 1943, the senior British representative in Washington (and also a close personal friend of General Marshall) to George Marshall, the Army chief of staff, to break the deadlock in January. And it took a thinly veiled threat from the British that continued opposition to Turing's visit could endanger further cooperation on the Enigma problem to finally turn the trick. On 9 January, after almost a month of wrangling, the acting chief of staff (Marshall had already left for Casablanca) informed the British that Turing's visit to Bell Labs had been approved.

Dill's intervention became possible, and effective, only because Tiltman was there, assuring both the senior British representative and the Americans that Enigma information was indeed flowing between the allies. His words to Dill were typical of his efforts:

"We make available to any properly accredited representative of the War Department all the processes and results of cryptographic investigation at the Government Code and Cypher School, but in the case of investigation on the higher planes of secrecy we have discouraged as far as possible the duplication of our work in the U.S.A. or elsewhere."

Of course, his "but" clause lay at the heart of the dispute. The U.S. Army did not want to play second fiddle on this issue. It wanted full access to not only the results of Enigma decryptions, but also the raw intercept and the bombes that made the decryptions possible. The Americans fully believed they could build a better bombe (which, in the case of the Navy, they wound up doing). Some of the British cryptographic leaders remained wedded to increasingly outdated concepts of security, and sought to keep the secrets of the bombes to themselves. Tiltman might have had to present their position to Dill and to the Americans, but it became increasingly clear during the war that he did not share their view. He pushed for full cooperation between the U.S. and British cryptologic services, a position he had taken up as early as 1941. Retrospectively, it is obvious that Tiltman was riding the wave of the future, and his efforts were instrumental in breaking down British reluctance to deal completely openly with the Americans. By 1943, largely through his persistence, an influx of Americans was arriving at Bletchley Park to reinforce the British, and to learn from their more experienced colleagues. After the war, he did not hesitate to point out the importance of this infusion of new blood.

Tiltman also recounted that it was during this visit in late 1942 and early 1943 that he almost met with General William Donovan, the head of the American Office of Strategic Services (OSS). A meeting of the two was arranged through Captain Hastings and Sir William Stevenson, who headed British security coordination and worked out of New York City. Tiltman traveled to New York and met Stevenson at the St. Regis Hotel. When told that Donovan wanted to talk to him, Tiltman agreed, but only if the discussion did not involve SIGINT exchanges between the Americans and the British. As Tiltman explained to Stevenson, he had just taken "a frightful beating" from Admiral Redman, and had been warned that he would remain a "friend" as long as he confined his dealings to the Army and the Navy. Redman was very clear that he should avoid having anything to do with "any other organizations." Based on that, Stevenson agreed to concoct a story about Tiltman missing connections to New York, and the meeting with Donovan never took place. It fell victim to the internecine feud between the established U.S. military cryptologic elements and the new kid on the block, the OSS.

Mission accomplished with regards to Turing, Tiltman returned to Britain in late January. As an aside to the whole imbroglio, Tiltman was asked years later if he had accompanied Turing to Bell Labs. He answered that he had not. In fact, he was never really sure what equipment Turing was supposed to inspect, and was sure he would not have understood it in any case. As for Turing, after overcoming a bit of unpleasantness when he was almost detained at Ellis Island because of insufficient documentation, he had spent the month during which he was the center of the storm with friends on Long Island, well away from the turmoil.

Back at Bletchley, Tiltman continued to devote his energies to attacking enemy ciphers, to securing British ones, and to fostering inter-Allied cooperation (especially with the Americans). Efforts to promote such cooperation were finally formalized through a series of agreements including the one between GC&CS and the U.S. Army signed on 17 May 1943 (the Travis-Strong Agreement, named after its two signatories). It, and an earlier agreement between the U.S. Navy and GC&CS, represented the beginning of a unique SIGINT agreement between foreign powers. Exchange of ideas, technology, and talent became a two-way street. Not only, as we have seen, did large numbers of Americans arrive at Bletchley, but a smaller, but still significant, number of Britons came to Washington to work with both the Army and Navy cryptologic services.

In spite of increasing administrative responsibilities, Tiltman did not forget his technical roots. He continued to assist, as time permitted, on sustained efforts against Japanese systems. Given British priorities, Japan had always taken a backseat to efforts against German cryptographic systems, and Japanese military codes and ciphers had lagged in importance behind Japanese naval ones. This picture began to change in 1943. The balance between Japanese systems changed somewhat at about this time. The disparity that had existed since before the war began between intercepts of Japanese naval and military communications had been largely rectified. As a result, the cryptanalysts began to have success against Japanese military codes and ciphers. Tiltman thought that the time was right to launch a more sustained and better-coordinated attack. He was instrumental in calling a conference at Bletchley of senior allied personnel working the Japanese systems. Agreement was reached to have the British concentrate on Japanese Army Air Force systems, while Arlington Hall would take over high-level systems used by Japanese ground forces. Central Bureau, a joint Australian-U.S.-UK effort working out of Australia, would work low-level military material.

By March 1944, Tiltman was back in Washington, this time accompanying Travis (head of GC&CS) and L. J. Hooper (head of the new Japanese Forces section which had been established in GC&CS after the Italian Armistice had made more staff available, and who would be director of GCHQ from 1965 to 1973) and others at a second conference on Japanese military codes. The expanding nature of the cooperation between the English-speaking allies was demonstrated by the fact that the British and Americans were joined this time by representatives from Canada and Australia.

Tiltman's efforts received de jure recognition by the British of the roles he had taken on during the war years. In the March 1944 reorganization he became one of the five deputy directors of GC&CS. In June he was promoted to brigadier (later many of his colleagues would be unable to remember exactly when he had officially been promoted, they could only ever remember calling him "the Brig"). These formal elevations did not, however, induce him to give up playing a significant role in the technical aspects of the business. In the summer of 1944 he was asked to turn his formidable powers against improvements that Japanese Navy had made to the JN-25 code they had used throughout the war. The Japanese had been alerted to the fact that their code might be exploitable by the rather injudicious use some American field commanders had been making of the intelligence provided to them. While a complete replacement of the code was logistically impossible given conditions the Japanese were operating under by 1944, they were able to implement security improvements. These changes led to a sixty percent loss of strategic intelligence, and the danger that Allied insight into Japanese naval order of battle was on the verge of becoming obsolete. Increased cooperation between the Americans and the British, and the efforts of people like Tiltman, eventually rectified the situation, and intelligence began to flow once again in a timely fashion.

Tiltman was back in the U.S. in late 1945, again with Travis, for negotiations to convert the wartime agreements into a document that would continue the relationship into the peace years. Unfortunately, the legacy of Enigma once more intervened. The U.S. hosts were headed by Admiral Redman, the same person who had attacked Tiltman over the perceived failure to be forthcoming with Enigma data in 1942.

Redman took the occasion to revisit the difficulties surrounding Enigma, and singled out Tiltman again as in some way responsible. What irritated Tiltman the most was that he knew that Redman was fully aware that it was largely through Tiltman's intervention that the impasse had been broken, in the Americans' favor. Tiltman held his fire during the session, but after it was over he told Travis that he refused to reenter the room as long as Redman remained in the chair. Every attempt by Travis to calm him down failed, and he withdrew from the negotiating process, depriving both sides of the benefit of his experience and wisdom.

## Postwar Experiences

With the war over, GC&CS became the Government Communications Headquarters (GCHQ) in 1946, and Tiltman was named an assistant director in 1947. He added one more "retirement" to his resumé, this one from the military (for the second time) the previous year. He was then named as the senior UK liaison officer (SUKLO) to the U.S. in 1949, working out of the British embassy in Washington until the next of his "retirements," this time his formal one from GCHQ in 1954, at the age of sixty. By special arrangement, and in recognition of his talents, he was allowed to continue working for GCHQ for another decade, including a stint as an integree at NSA from 1958 to 1964, finally stepping down from British service at the age of seventy in 1964.

During this period of his life, he became interested in one of the more puzzling items in the long history of cryptology, the *Voynich Manuscript*. This book, which now resides in the Yale University Library, is claimed by some to have been written by the thirteenth century English scholar Roger Bacon. More likely, it was written in the late sixteenth or early seventeenth century and attributed to Roger Bacon in an attempt to embellish its mystique, and to drive up the price that was asked of the Holy Roman Emperor, Rudolph II, an inveterate yet gullible book collector. It is a combination of an unknown script and colored pictures that appear to represent plants, astrological or cosmological material, pharmaceutical recipes, and human figures surrounded by bizarre objects.

It has attracted the attention of numerous cryptanalysts, with the two most prominent being Tiltman himself and William Friedman. It is perhaps no mystery why men of their talents would be drawn to a text that one would assume had meaning. Friedman seems to have caught the bug first and drew Tiltman's attention to it in about 1951. Friedman devoted sporadic interest to it until his death in 1969, while Tiltman's interest seemed to wane sometime in the 1970s. Neither of them arrived at a solution, but then again, neither has anyone else. One could speculate that if two of the greatest cryptologic minds of the twentieth century could not unravel the mystery of the manuscript, then perhaps there really is nothing there to unravel, and the *Voynich Manuscript* is nothing more than a hoax.

Tiltman's contributions to the cryptologic world, and to UK-U.S. SIGINT relations, did not end with his "retirement" in 1964. He moved to the U.S. to be closer to his daughter, and became a consultant to NSA. Ironically, it took special intervention by the director of the Agency for this "foreigner" to clear the security hurdles, and fortunately sanity prevailed. He lent his expertise to working a number of hand systems still in use in a number of Eastern European and Third World countries.

His years at NSA were used by GCHQ to help smooth over a potential problem that came in the form of a soon-to-be-published book. In 1966 a relative newcomer to the world of cryptologic writing, David Kahn, was preparing to release his groundbreaking book *The Codebreakers*. Prepublication hints of what the book would contain caused considerable consternation among the cryptologic services on both sides of the Atlantic. Tiltman was asked by GCHQ to approach Kahn and get him to remove any reference to itself, its location, or its director. The negotiations were successful, so when the book appeared in 1967 it was met with a great deal more equipoise in the UK than greeted it in the U.S.

He also recounted a second encounter with Kahn, this time when Kahn tried to interview him as a source for his writings. Kahn singled out Tiltman as the top technical man in the field, but the Brig would not budge from his position that his view of what was required of him because of his oaths to maintain security precluded him from being connected with any attempt to reveal the secrets which he had learned over a lifetime of service. He would make it clear, however, that he bore no ill will towards Kahn, and indeed had cooperated with him when the subject had turned to Tiltman's work on the *Voynich Manuscript*.

He did not feel the same way towards others who chose to write about cryptanalytic efforts that he had been involved in, especially when he considered that those writers were bound, as he believed himself to be, by an oath to preserve the secrecy of their endeavors. He felt this oath was a lifetime obligation, not one to be laid aside at the time of retirement. He was particularly critical of the work of F. W. Winterbotham, the former SIS officer who first revealed the Enigma story in the mid-1970s. Tiltman knew that Winterbotham's book, *The Ultra Secret*, was riddled with inaccuracies.

Not the least of these is the myth that Churchill had received warning through Enigma exploitation that the Germans had planned a large-scale air raid against the city of Coventry in early November 1940. The myth maintains that, to protect British exploitation of Enigma, Churchill refused to allow the city to be warned or evacuated. Just on the surface, there are several flaws with this story. First, all British cities were aware in 1940 that they might be the targets of German air raids. Second, evacuating an urban area would likely have caused more problems than it solved. The impact of Hurricanes Katrina and Rita in the U.S. in 2005 more than demonstrates the difficulties that result from attempts to evacuate large urban areas, even with twenty-first century technology. What lay behind the myth involved British exploitation of another piece of German technology, namely the beam system the German air force used to guide their bombers to their targets. The British were able, before the Coventry raid, to intercept part of the beam system, but they needed to know the intersection point (that is, where the Germans would release their bombs) of the beams, as well as the frequencies being used to transmit them. The intersection point became known on the afternoon of the raid, and British scientist R. V. Jones correctly surmised the frequencies. Jamming efforts failed, however, because the Germans used sophisticated filters that enabled their systems to ignore the jamming signal.

More damaging in the Brig's eyes was the precedent set by the work, which opened the floodgates for others to publish works on subjects he felt should have been kept from public sight, at least until fully documented histories could be officially released by scholars who had complete access to the information. He felt that to allow the Winterbothams of the world free rein was to make a mockery of the hundreds who went to their graves keeping the secrets they had sworn to keep.

## Insights on Cryptology

During his years at NSA, Tiltman continued his life-long efforts to educate those who would take up the task once he finally, finally set it down. In doing so, he laid down a number of principles for cryptographic security that have enduring value, decades after he stated what has since become the obvious. These were lessons learned over a lifetime of devoted service:

- Any cipher system is a compromise between security and practicability.

- Responsibility for the security of a system has to be taken completely out of the hands of the cipher operator. It has to be proof against attempts by holders to circumvent instructions through laziness.

- A system is only as strong as its weakest link. Cryptanalysts make their living out of the sloppy thinking and enthusiastic over-ingenuity of designers. The possible damage from compromise has to be taken into account when the system is assessed, in advance of its use.

- All transposition systems are dangerous. They are vulnerable to special circumstances thrown up by chance, and it is difficult for the designer to eliminate such possibilities absolutely.

- Usage of a system should be periodically monitored to ensure it is not being overloaded.

- Many systems have been ruined by reliance for security on variant substitution units.

- Tailing and trailing are used to ensure even overall use of long, though limited key.

❏ Stereotyped openings and signatures are often unavoidable. Security is achieved by bisection or by the use of a separate system for stereotyped material.

❏ Otherwise secure systems will be ruined by inadequate indicating systems.

❏ It may take only one bust to ruin security of an otherwise sound system.

❏ One-time pads don't have to be absolutely random, just unpredictable.

❏ Ciphers have to be specially designed for proforma reports.

❏ It is the absolute responsibility of experienced cryptanalysts to pass on their knowledge. [Tiltman had no use for those who create an aura of mystery around their work to enhance their own importance.]

❏ The most badly documented aspect of work against a cipher system is the initial break-in. This documentation usually occurs well after the event, and details are often forgotten.

Tiltman consistently maintained that the justification for the effort put into SIGINT (always a very expensive venture) is that it is a weapon of defense. He insisted that, in addition to attacking the sophisticated systems of opponents, less sophisticated systems and the systems used by less important states should not be ignored. This stemmed from his belief that SIGINT is relatively cheap only if it can be carried out as expeditiously as possible, and that means gaining insight into a country's cryptologic practices early on in the game. It also meant recognizing that information derived from less sophisticated systems could often prove useful as cribs for breaking into the more sophisticated ones.

Further, speed of thinking and speed of operation were essential in this process; otherwise, the intelligence gathered would be dated and not worth the price paid at all. All of this required a breadth and depth of experience, factors he felt were being increasingly neglected in the development of budding cryptanalysts, a neglect he feared would have future, negative repercussions.

As he spent time reflecting on his long career, Tiltman was able to admit to having fallen victim to a certain amount of parochial thinking that clouded his approach to organizing GCHQ just before the end of the war. He had been, and at heart remained, a cryptanalyst. He admitted that, as a result, he had come to have little appreciation for the contributions other skills, particularly traffic analysis, could bring to the table. In later years he regretted that shortsightedness, especially as he watched cryptographic systems become increasingly complex and unbreakable, a situation that called more and more for the attributes of the traffic analyst to be brought to bear.

## End of Career/Legacy

Throughout Tiltman's career, his contributions were acknowledged and rewarded by both the U.S. and Great Britain. In 1930 he was made on Officer of the Order of the British Empire (OBE), and was advanced to a Commander of the British Empire (CBE) in 1944. To this was added the honor of Companion of the Order of St. Michael and St. George (CMG) in 1954. On this side of the Atlantic, he was honored with the Legion of Merit in 1946. Some of his contemporaries expressed surprise in later years that he was never knighted by the British monarch, but he was not high enough in the hierarchy to warrant that distinction (only the director of GC&CS was so honored).

The Brig finally really retired in 1980, after sixty-six years of singular service to two nations; sixty of those years were devoted to cryptologic work where his insights and innovations benefited both the cryptographic and cryptanalytic disciplines. He moved to Hawaii, again to be near his daughter, and passed away in 1982. He stands among the giants of cryptology, a status NSA acknowledged by placing him in its Hall of Honor in 2004.

The legacy Tiltman left is a large one. From breaking Russian diplomatic and Comintern systems in the 1920s and 1930s, he moved on to seminal efforts against Japanese military and naval systems in the 1930s and 1940s. To these accomplishments he added the insight that made exploitation of major German systems such as Tunny possible. His skills were not limited to the exploitation of systems used by his country's foes, but extended to the other side of the cryptologic mission. The systems he created to protect British and allied signals provided reliable and much-needed security. He continued after the war, through the 1950s, 1960s, and 1970s, to successfully attack systems devised by countries considered to be of national interest to both Great Britain and the U.S. No less importantly, he helped cement relations between the U.S. and his native Britain, a partnership that continues to benefit both nations.

To these technical and partner-building skills he added personal attributes of integrity and loyalty and a keen, almost fierce, desire to impart his skills to the young. He sought to inspire them to a level of success they otherwise would have thought unattainable. It was not hyperbole when Sir Brian Tovey, director of GCHQ, praised Tiltman as one of the greatest cryptanalysts Great Britain has ever produced. His long list of accomplishments deserves no less an accolade.

John F. Clabby
Center for Cryptologic History

Printed in Great Britain
by Amazon